SHARKS

LIVING WILD

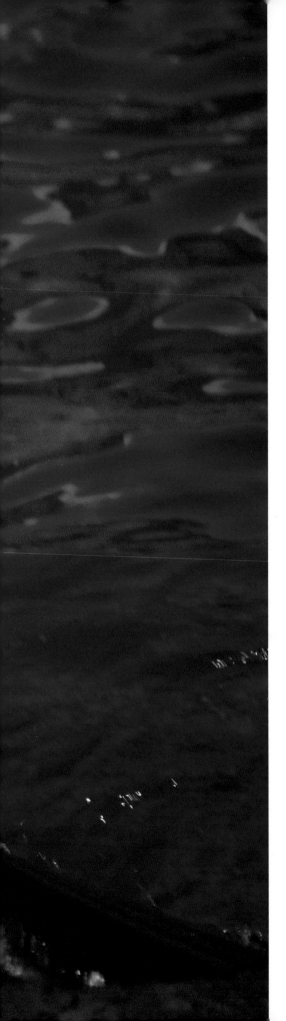

LIVING WILD

Published by Creative Education

P.O. Box 227, Mankato, Minnesota 56002

Creative Education is an imprint of The Creative Company

www.thecreativecompany.us

Design and production by Mary Herrmann

Art direction by Rita Marshall

Printed in the United States of America

Photographs by 123RF (cbpix, Judy Picciotto), Alamy (Mark Conlin, Martin Shields, Stephen Frink Collection, Visual & Written SL), Corbis (Ralph A. Clevenger, Stephen Frink, Amos Nachoum), Dreamstime (Catman73, Chrismoncrieff, Cphoto, Ironrodart, Johan63, Michaeljung, Qldian), Getty Images (Thomas J. Abercrombie/ National Geographic, Awashima Marine Park, Brandon Cole, David Doubilit/National Geographic, Georgette Douwma, Roger Horrocks, Steven Hunt, BRIAN J. SKERRY, Raul Touzon), iStockphoto (Chuck Babbitt, Chris Dascher, Keith Flood, Anton Leyland, John Stublar, Klaas Lingbeek van Kranen), Minden Pictures (Fred Bavendam)

Library of Congress Cataloging-in-Publication Data

Gish, Melissa.

Sharks / by Melissa Gish.

p. cm. — (Living wild)

Includes bibliographical references and index.

ISBN 978-1-58341-742-3

1. Sharks—Juvenile literature. I. Title. II. Series.

QL638.9.G57 2009

597.3—dc22   2008009505

First Edition

9 8 7 6 5 4 3 2 1

CREATIVE EDUCATION

SHARKS

Melissa Gish

The sun shines through wispy clouds,
warming the ocean. A shadow appears

underwater, and a gray fin the length of a
person's arm cuts through the waves.

The sun shines through wispy clouds, warming the ocean. A shadow appears underwater, and a gray fin the length of a person's arm cuts through the waves. Following the scent of bloody fish bait, a great white shark surfaces. As the bait is pulled closer to a boat, the shark instinctively follows. Suddenly, the shark finds itself trapped and hoisted from the water in a metal cradle the size of a small car. Veterinarians and scientists immediately leap onto the shark's back. The shark could thrash suddenly, tossing the researchers into the sea. It could twist its body and bite off the arms of its captors—but it doesn't. Incredibly, it lies still and allows the scientists to attach a small electronic tag to its back fin. After receiving a shot of medicine to help it recover, the shark is released into the sea to begin transmitting information that may someday reveal its secrets.

WHERE IN THE WORLD THEY LIVE

■ **Wobbegong**
western Pacific Ocean and eastern Indian Ocean, around Indonesia and Australia

□ **Lemon Shark**
along subtropical and tropical Atlantic coastlines of North and South America

■ **Whitetip Reef Shark**
around coral reefs in Indian and Pacific oceans

■ **Great White Shark**
coastal waters in all major oceans, especially off the southern coasts of Australia, Africa, and California

More than 350 shark species inhabit parts of all the world's oceans. Some species frequent the shallow waters near coastlines, while others seek out the deeper waters of the open sea. The colored squares represent common locations of eight shark species.

■ **Tiger Shark**
tropical and temperate waters of all oceans, especially around islands in the central Pacific

■ **Hammerhead Shark**
worldwide in warm coastal waters

■ **Nurse Shark**
western Atlantic coastline from Rhode Island to Brazil, eastern Pacific from Baja California to Peru, eastern Atlantic coastline of central Africa

■ **Whale Shark**
tropical and temperate waters of the open seas

PERFECT PREDATORS

Named for its gills with frilled edges, the rare frilled shark lives in waters up to a mile (1.6 km) deep.

Sharks are some of the most diverse fish in the sea and some of the oldest fish on the planet. They inhabit all of Earth's oceans—even the waters around Antarctica. Sharks belong to the class Chondrichthyes. This is a group of jawed fish whose skeletons are made of **cartilage** instead of bone. Nearly 400 different species of shark have been discovered and named—the latest two as recently as 2006. Sharks and their closest relatives, skates and rays, are in the subclass Elasmobranchii and are commonly called elasmobranchs.

About 30 million years ago, the various shark species **evolved** to develop the hinged top jaws and nictitating (*NIK-ti-tayt-ing*) membranes (see-through inner eyelids) that are the characteristics of modern sharks. Only the frilled sharks have retained certain primitive features similar to their ancestors: These eel-like, deep-sea dwellers have an upper jaw that is part of the skull, and they do not have nictitating membranes.

Differences in jaw placement, body and fin shapes, and behavior show how each shark species has

At 52 feet (16 m) long and weighing 48 tons (44 t), *Carcharadon megalodon* was Earth's largest fish. It disappeared two million years ago.

adapted to a particular way of life. General physical characteristics also determine how scientists divide sharks into eight orders. Size has less to do with groupings than does the shape of a shark's jaws and fins. For example, the order known as mackerel sharks contains both the basking shark, which reaches lengths of up to 40 feet (12.2 m), as well as the goblin shark, whose maximum length is 12 feet (3.7 m).

Sharks must live in salt water, but some, such as the Irrawaddy river shark, frequent **brackish** rivers and **estuaries**. Hammerheads and tiger sharks favor tropical ocean waters warmer than 70 °F (21 °C). Sand tiger sharks, thresher sharks, and dogfish prefer temperate waters between 50 and 70 °F (10 to 21 °C). And any waters colder than 50 °F (10 °C) are home to frilled and goblin sharks. The sleeper shark has even been known to live under large areas of floating ice near the North and South poles.

Found in oceans worldwide, the well-known great white shark hunts both at the surface and at depths of 1,000 feet (305 m). Great whites can grow to be 20 feet (6 m) long and can weigh 5,000 pounds (2,268 kg). Yet

The southern stingray may be
related to sharks, but it is also prey
for hammerheads and lemon sharks.

Whale sharks migrate every spring to the central part of Australia's western coast to feed on coral.

the great white is surpassed in size by the whale shark, the giant of the deep and the largest fish on the planet. A whale shark can measure more than 40 feet (12.2 m) long and weigh more than 20 tons (18 t). However, fewer than 20 percent of all shark species grow larger than 5 feet (1.5 m) in length. One of the smallest species, the pygmy shark, is slightly more than 10 inches (25 cm) long.

Each shark species has adapted to life in a specific water depth. For example, the coloring of most bottom-dwelling sharks is dark and spotted like the sandy ocean floor. This provides **camouflage** for such bottom-dwellers as angelsharks and wobbegongs (also called carpet sharks) to snatch unsuspecting prey. Other sharks are colored bright blue, gray, or silvery white to blend into the colors of their open-sea habitat.

Most bony fishes have a swim bladder, a gas-filled sac or pouch that regulates a fish's **buoyancy**, keeping it afloat when it isn't moving. Sharks do not have swim bladders, though. If they stop swimming, they will sink. Like all fish, sharks breathe through slits in their bodies called gills. A shark must swim continuously with its mouth open to breathe. Water is forced backward over the gills, where thin membranes collect oxygen and transfer it to the shark's bloodstream. Bottom-dwelling species of shark are the exception; not only can they rest on the ocean floor, but they can continue breathing

Male sharks are identified by the two reproductive organs, called claspers, located on the underside of the body near the tail.

Despite the scary, ragged-toothed appearance of the sand tiger shark, divers do not consider it to be a threat.

there by using small slits behind each eye called spiracles to pump water over their gills.

A unique characteristic that elasmobranchs share is their denticle-covered skin. Instead of scales, sharks, skates, and rays have denticles, or toothlike projections that all point in the same direction. The sleek skin offers the least resistance to the water flowing over it as the shark swims. This helps sharks move silently and more quickly than their prey.

A shark's most valuable feature is its teeth, which appear in distinctive sizes and shapes, depending on the species. For example, great white, tiger, and dusky sharks have wide, wedge-shaped teeth with jagged edges. These teeth are designed to rip chunks of meat from prey. Wobbegongs and various reef sharks have thin, knife-shaped teeth to catch and hold fish that are then swallowed whole. Some sharks, such as nurse sharks and angelsharks, have flattened teeth that are used to crush shellfish.

Shark teeth are arranged in rows, with most sharks having 5 rows of 20 to 50 teeth each. Every one to two weeks, as teeth are broken or worn down, replacement teeth move forward. Some sharks may go through as many as 50,000 teeth in a lifetime. Shark teeth contain the mineral compound calcium hydroxyapatite. This is the same substance found in human and animal teeth and bones.

Sharks have five different kinds of fins. Two pectoral fins behind the gills are used for vertical movement and steering. A pair of pelvic fins on the lower body keep sharks from rolling over, and the caudal, or tail, fin helps a shark propel forward. One or two dorsal fins (or spines in some species) on the back also stabilize the shark. The anal fin near the tail provides extra stability for certain species. Sharks can maneuver quickly, but they cannot stop abruptly or back up.

Tiny pores called the ampullae of Lorenzini look like dark spots on the face and are special sensory organs. They allow sharks to detect differences in **electromagnetic** signals, such as those made by injured fish or by other sharks while feeding. A shark's skin also contains many pores that lead to small sense organs inside its body called lateral line organs. These organs tell the shark when to speed up, slow down, change direction, and right itself in the water.

Sharks' teeth start growing before birth. While examining a pregnant sand tiger shark in 1982, biologist Stewart Springer was bitten by an unborn pup.

Great hammerhead sharks, the largest of the nine hammerheads, eat together but disperse when darkness falls.

INCREDIBLE VARIETY

Instinct seems to compel some shark species, including the great hammerhead, to gather in schools to feed. Cow sharks have been known to hunt cooperatively in packs to kill seals and dolphins. Other sharks, such as great whites and tiger sharks, are solitary. However, the search for food is a shark's strongest instinct, and sharks do little more day and night than patrol the seas in search of food. They must consume two percent of their body weight per day to survive. Researchers are still trying to determine whether sharks truly sleep, as studies have shown them to appear ever watchful for prey.

Smaller sharks typically remain in areas where food is abundant, such as coral reefs, but most shark species will circle the Earth's oceans to hunt. Many follow seasonal migration routes of fish or gather along coasts, where vulnerable newborn seals and sea lions first take to the water. Sharks are ambush predators, rushing up from beneath prey animals to strike. A shark can stalk its prey for miles and detect blood from up to three miles (4.8 km) away using its twin nasal sacs, which are lined with a

A large shark will raise its head out of the water around seal colonies to check out the prey. This action is called a "spy hop."

French grunts (above) school together for protection from predators such as the Caribbean reef shark (opposite).

sensitive tissue. Its scent detection is so powerful that a shark can steer its way along a scent trail in total darkness.

Sharks swallow their food whole instead of chewing it. They eat mainly fish but also prey on mammals such as sea lions. To eat larger animals, they must rip off chunks of meat before gulping it down. This behavior leads to a unique activity among sharks called a "feeding frenzy." Because sharks generally do not defend a territory against intruders, sharks of different species will often feed together. As sharks gather to feed, they sometimes rise into a "frenzy," becoming more and more agitated and biting wildly at anything and everything within reach— even other sharks.

Most sharks are fussy eaters. They prefer fatty foods and will usually spit out anything that isn't nutritious. This is why most humans who are bitten by sharks are not devoured—humans are not a shark's favorite meal. Death from a shark bite is usually the result of blood loss, and very few people who are bitten by a shark are eaten. A floating, blubbery whale carcass, on the other hand, may provide food for several days or weeks.

Although sharks are compelled to search for food by instinct, some species are believed to be highly intelligent. One example is the whale shark. Researchers have observed whale sharks exhibiting curious, gentle behavior around human divers that is reminiscent of dolphin

A whale shark's jaws are lined with 300 rows of pinhead-sized teeth that are used to scoop in tiny fish.

behavior. In addition, while most captive sharks simply become agitated around feeding time, whale sharks learn to calmly position themselves so that keepers can pour food into their mouths at regular times of the day.

Whale sharks survive by eating plankton and krill, organisms that can be found in great numbers, drifting like giant ribbons in the sea or floating near the water's surface. Whale sharks can eat 5,200 pounds (2,359 kg) of these tiny creatures every day by sifting them from the water. The other two filter feeders, which are also harmless to humans, are basking and megamouth sharks. The deep-sea megamouth shark was first identified about 30 years ago and has been spotted fewer than 40 times since then.

Little is known about shark reproduction. Some shark species may mate once a year, while others may mate only once every two to three years. Sharks have slow **metabolisms** and do not mature as quickly as other fish. Most shark species begin mating by age six. However, lemon sharks do not breed until they are 12, and white-spotted spurdogs must be 20. While most bony fish produce millions of eggs in a season, sharks produce far fewer live offspring, which are called pups. Depending on the species, **gestation** lasts from five months to two years. The number of pups born at one time can be as few as 2 or, in the case of the whale shark, as many as 300.

Each species of shark gives birth in one of three ways. A viviparous shark carries its young inside its body; it then gives birth to fully formed offspring in a way that is similar to how mammals give birth. An oviparous shark

Atlanta's Georgia Aquarium is the only facility outside Asia to house whale sharks. The sharks are kept in a 6.3-million-gallon (24 million l) tank.

lays egg cases that contain developing baby sharks. The rectangular cases are laid among coral reefs or beds of water plants so that they can become anchored. Their coloring camouflages them, providing protection from predators. When each young shark is fully developed, it breaks out of the egg case. An ovoviviparous shark carries eggs containing the young inside its body. The eggs hatch while still inside the mother, but then the babies continue to grow until they are strong enough to leave her body.

A number of shark species practice oophagy, an activity in which a developing shark feeds on its siblings while still inside the mother's body. This means that fewer offspring are born, but because they begin life as the strongest and most aggressive pups, these offspring will have the best chance of survival. Research has determined that shark pups develop their fins and open their eyes a month before leaving their eggs. Most sharks that are either born live or hatched from eggs are already fully formed and immediately ready to search for prey. In their eagerness to begin life as miniature versions of their predatory parents, newborn sharks have been known to attack fish larger than themselves.

A few species of shark, such as lemon sharks, linger around their newborns for several weeks to keep predators away. But generally, pups are left completely on their own. A shark's greatest natural threat is being eaten by a bigger shark, so juvenile sharks tend to stay in shallow coastal waters or among coral reefs until they grow large enough to avoid being considered prey. The exact life span of sharks is unknown, but most species are thought to live between 20 and 30 years. Continued research to better understand the life cycle of sharks is crucial to the protection of shark populations in the wild.

Most egg cases, such as this swell shark egg case, resemble ocean plants and are shaped like pillows.

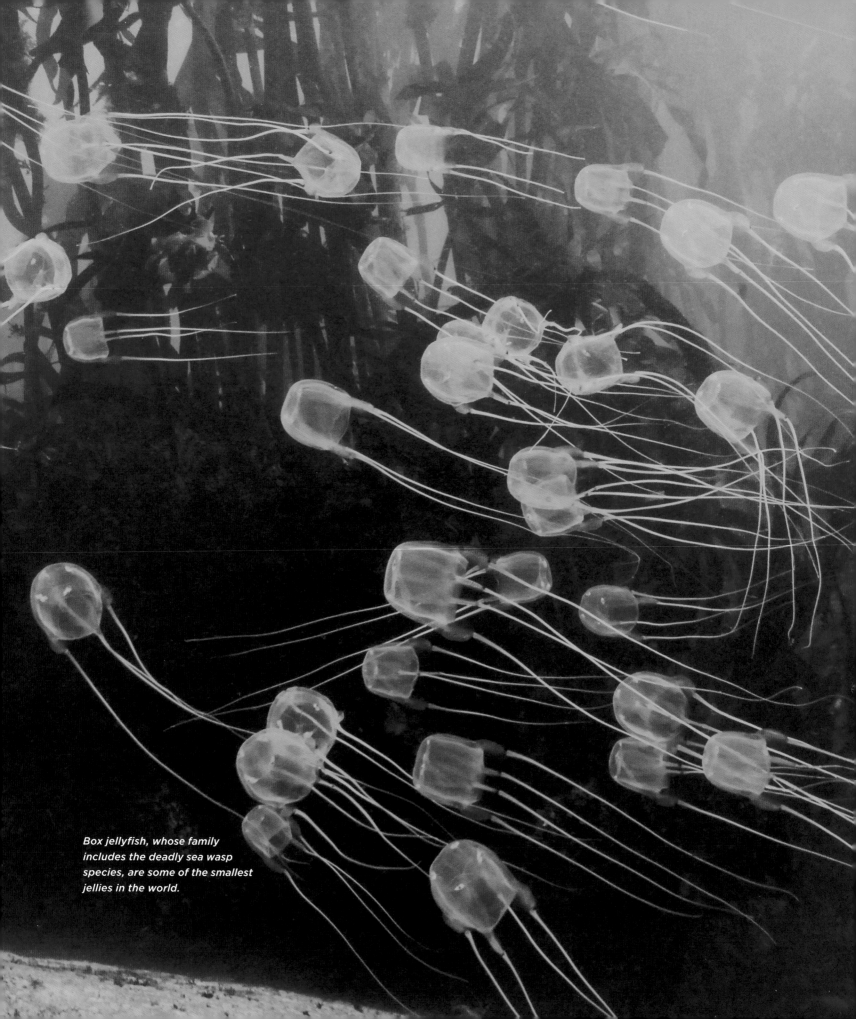

Box jellyfish, whose family includes the deadly sea wasp species, are some of the smallest jellies in the world.

A BAD REPUTATION

F ew animals on the planet are more feared by humans than sharks. However, not all sharks deserve to be feared. In fact, fewer than 20 percent of shark species are considered dangerous to humans. Despite popular belief, the great white is not the most dangerous shark. Tiger sharks will eat almost anything and are responsible for more deadly encounters with humans than are great whites. And certain jellyfish pose more of a threat to people who swim in the seas and oceans. Children who have been stung by the box jellyfish have died within minutes of being stung. Bees, wasps, and snakes are also responsible for more human deaths than sharks are. Between 50 and 75 shark attacks occur each year; on average, only 8 to 12 of those incidents are fatal.

Most shark encounters that are called "attacks" are, in fact, not instances of aggressive behavior. Sharks are not naturally interested in eating humans; however, if they come across something that looks like it might be food—including humans—they will instinctively taste it. And blood will automatically catch a shark's interest. If a

Most sharks cruise at 1 to 3 miles (1.6–4.8 km) per hour, but they can reach speeds of up to 18 miles (29 km) per hour for short periods.

Helicoprion, a shark that lived about 250 million years ago, had teeth that grew from its jaw in a coiled whorl.

swimmer scrapes his foot on a rock, for example, a shark will detect the blood and, thinking it has located food, seek out the swimmer.

Some people have no fear of sharks, though. Sharks are important figures in native Hawaiian tradition. Some Hawaiian tribes worshiped sharks as *aumakua*, or family gods. These people believed that some of their ancestors took the form of sharks after death and protected the person who dreamed about them. Many native Hawaiians also believed in a shark god named Kamohoali'i and called "The shark that walks upright." Other tribes hunted fierce great white and tiger sharks for their teeth, skin, and other useful body parts. In 1778, British explorer James Cook was the first European to visit the Hawaiian Islands. He collected from the native people various tools and weapons made with sharks' teeth, as well as drumheads made from sharkskin.

Captain Cook also traveled to the islands of Tonga, whose people have always valued sharks as a food source. Today, the fishing ritual of "shark calling" is still practiced in Tonga. Fishermen shake a coconut rattle above the water's surface and sing a traditional

shark-calling song. Drawn by the sound, sharks begin to appear. Then the fishermen beat the water with sticks and chant "*Vili pea hoko*," meaning "others to follow," to lure more sharks. Finally, the sharks are captured using live bait. When the fishermen return home, all the villagers feast on the shark meat.

In the Fiji Islands, early 20th-century explorers witnessed the practice of "kissing the shark." Fishermen

Many sharks cruise shallow waters less than 100 feet (30 m) deep in search of seals and other prey.

captured a shark in a net, then turned it over on its back to kiss its belly. The Fijians believed that kissing a shark would protect fishermen. Pairs of shark charmers on the island of Sri Lanka still perform rituals believed to protect pearl divers from sharks. One charmer locks himself in a room and chants, while the other dives into the sea and casts a spell to drive sharks away from divers who collect oysters from the seabed.

Fishermen in Vietnam revere the whale shark and call it Ca Ong, or Sir Fish. To this day, altars used for requesting Ca Ong's protection are still built in the sand dunes along the central and southern Vietnamese coast. Nearby, in Japan, sighting a whale shark is considered to be a sign of good luck, even though the Japanese hunt the sharks for food.

When European explorers such as Amerigo Vespucci, Vasco da Gama, and Ferdinand Magellan set sail more than 500 years ago, they recorded their encounters with giant sea monsters, which were most likely whales and sharks. These stories captured people's imaginations, and sharks became the victims of misconceptions that have persisted for generations. In 1947, scuba-diving pioneer

Hans Hass made a film called *Men among Sharks*. It gave most people their first images of sharks in the wild.

Widespread public attention was turned to sharks in 1974, when author Peter Benchley wrote *Jaws*. After hearing about a fisherman who caught a 20-foot (6 m) great white shark, Benchley wondered what would happen if a fish like that moved into the waters of a tourist resort and refused to leave. The following year, director Steven Spielberg made the film *Jaws*, which sparked a widespread irrational fear of sharks. The film also prompted people to take up the sport of shark hunting—a practice that has increased in recent decades.

Sharks are also hunted around the world for their use in consumer products. Shark liver contains an oil that is used in cosmetics, lubricants, and paint base. The cartilage is used in many traditional alternative medicines. Additionally, cooked shark meat and fins are growing in popularity in some countries. Scientists estimate that 100 million sharks are killed every year.

Unfortunately, irresponsible hunting practices such as finning (when fishermen take only the fins of sharks) are resulting in the reduction of many shark species. After a

Few laws protect sharks from being caught by sport fishermen and commercial fisheries that use bait.

shark is caught, its fins are sliced off, and the shark is then dumped back into the sea, either dead already or doomed to die because it cannot swim. Its fins are usually sold to restaurants or markets for use in a dish called shark fin soup.

One person who tried to promote a change in people's perceptions about sharks was, ironically, Peter Benchley. The man who made a fortune on the horror created by *Jaws* changed his viewpoint about sharks the year following the film's release. He became a vocal supporter of shark conservation and wrote a number of nonfiction books about sharks to help people understand that all sharks do not deserve to be feared. Benchley was also a spokesman for the Environmental Defense Fund's campaign to end the overhunting of sharks.

Each year, the World Conservation Union compiles a "Red List" of endangered animals. More than 100 shark species appear on the current list, including several angelsharks, the great white and great hammerhead, the gentle basking shark, and more than a dozen varieties of catsharks. Some species, such as the Ganges shark, striped dogfish, and the Bizant river shark, are critically endangered and could face **extinction** within the next decade.

The mako shark is the fastest shark. Some makos have been recorded swimming for short bursts at up to 60 miles (96 km) per hour.

A shark's prominent dorsal fin can be in danger of being cut off by fishermen who practice finning.

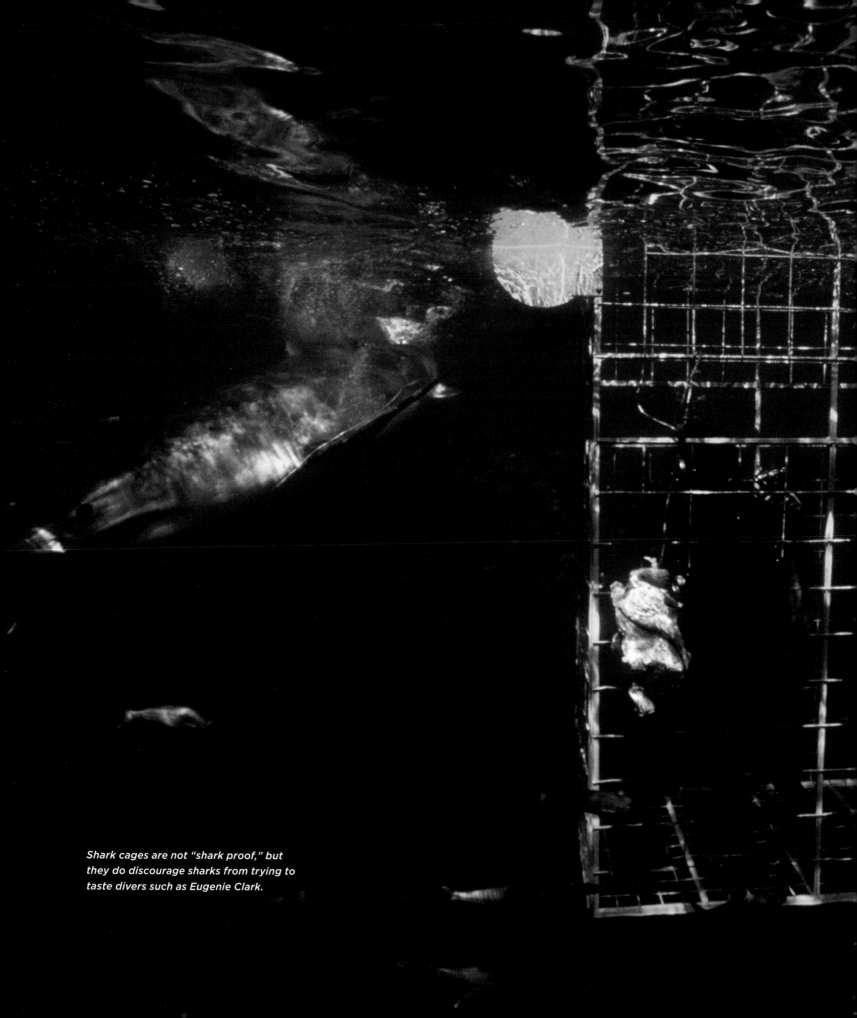

Shark cages are not "shark proof," but they do discourage sharks from trying to taste divers such as Eugenie Clark.

REVEALING MYSTERIES

R elatively little is known about sharks because, until recently, few in-depth shark research projects were conducted. In addition, prior to 1975, sharks were considered to have little **commercial** value. But as populations of fish that had traditionally supplied food around the world began to decline, sharks, which were plentiful, began to appeal more and more to fisheries. More efficient methods of fishing for sharks were developed, and soon, sharks were being harvested at an alarming rate. In just a short time, populations of many shark species plummeted.

Shark research is not a new field, but it continues to expand, and the public's understanding of sharks grows with it. Long before wildlife conservationist Steve Irwin's show *Crocodile Hunter* made close encounters with dangerous animals popular on television, French **oceanographer** Jacques-Yves Cousteau, American shark researcher Eugenie Clark, and Australian underwater experts Rod and Valerie Taylor were writing books and making documentary films about swimming with sharks.

Jacques Cousteau began his career in the French navy, but he became known for his studies of sea life.

Cousteau was a champion of shark conservation. He and a French engineer invented SCUBA gear to better enable people to study sharks and other sea creatures. Clark, who was known as "the shark lady," began studying sharks in the 1960s. Among her many contributions to the field was her research that led to the development of various types of shark repellent.

Early observations of sharks were done from a "shark cage" by divers who baited sharks to get them to come close. The cage that researchers commonly use to study sharks in the wild was originally designed in the 1960s by naturalist-photographer Peter Gimbel. He called his invention the Blue Meridian Diver's Elevator. It had its own buoyancy system that allowed it to go up or down at a selected speed and hover at a particular depth.

Underwater photographer Rod Taylor and his wife Valerie, a champion spearfisher, became concerned over the threat to sharks when shark fishing increased in the 1970s. Their studies led to improvements in safety cages and protective gear. The Taylors spent a decade developing a chain-mail suit similar to that of a medieval knight's, which resists many forms of shark bites. Valerie

HONORING KAMOHO, THE SHARK THAT WALKS UPRIGHT

Restless is the island Kuaihelani

Overwhelmed by raging desires

The turbulent abode of the shark that walks upright

Soaring silently in the horizon beyond

The wings of Honua-ia-kea totter about

A vessel flaunting amongst a mirage

Paddled along by the voyaging companions

Keaukai (the tide), and Keaumiki (the current)

The prominent line seen

From the dorsal that split the surface of the sea

Is the fluttering path of Kamohoali'i

Sailing on to verdant islands

Steer now to Nihoa

An island shaken by the sea

Steer on to Ka'ula

An island reached by canoe

Turn now the bow of the canoe towards Ni'ihau

Kamohoali'i steers again

Steer on to Kaua'i

Once more to O'ahu

Skillful is the helmsman Kamohoali'i

Steer now to Maui

Once more to Hawai'i

To a new home in lush spires

Honoring Kamoho, the shark that walks upright.

Mark Keali'i Ho'omalu

Sharks have a symbiotic relationship with remoras, the small fish that clean their skin in return for eating scraps of sharks' prey.

successfully tested the suit herself, allowing blue sharks to bite her protected arms and hands.

By 1980, other conservationists and researchers had rallied to the sharks' cause. Now, hundreds of organizations throughout the world study sharks so they can educate the general public as well as lawmakers, who need to better manage shark-fishing industries. Information that scientists are now discovering is also used to understand how sharks function in the global **ecosystem** and to identify ways that sharks may even provide medical resources for humans.

Researchers today have found that, by staying out of the water and not interfering with sharks' activities, they can get a more accurate picture of normal shark behavior. Every day, scientists from the Pelagic Shark Research Foundation board boats to observe great white sharks feeding on seals, sea lions, and other animals off the coast of California. This "hands-off" research provides a clearer picture of how great whites behave in the wild.

Other scientists insist on taking a more hands-on approach. One type of research involves capturing tiger

sharks and attaching small cameras to their bodies. Conceived in 1986 by marine biologist Greg Marshall, the Crittercam device transmits images from the shark's point of view. Crittercams have been used on numerous sea and land animals with great success.

Scientists with the Wildlife Conservation Society in New York conduct research on great whites off the coast of South Africa by capturing them and hoisting them out of the water in large cradles for short periods of time to fit them

Like all hammerheads, the scalloped hammerhead's eyes and nostrils are located on either side of its head.

Whitetip reef sharks, also known as blunthead sharks, rest in the crevices of coral reefs throughout the Pacific Ocean.

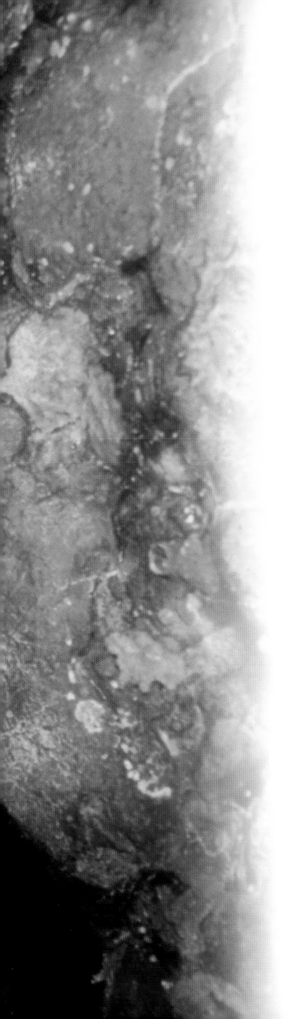

with **satellite** tags. The movement of the sharks can then be tracked and recorded by a satellite-computer system. No harm comes to the shark, and the data gained is invaluable.

Satellite tracking is a fairly new technology, but a similar program in the Florida Keys has been going on for many years. Scientists capture nurse sharks by net to study them. They check to see if each shark already has a tag, and if it doesn't, they tag it. They also attach "pingers" to some sharks; these devices send out radio signals. The sharks are cleaned of any fishing hooks or **parasites**, and then they are weighed and measured. Also, a small piece of fin is taken to test the shark's **DNA**. This is done so that scientists can keep track of how tagged sharks are related to one another. The sharks are then released into the sea until the next year.

Studies on sharks' intelligence are often conducted as well. Some lemon sharks and sand tiger sharks, for example, have been trained by researchers to perform certain behaviors in response to certain sounds. Lemon sharks have proven that they can learn faster and remember such **conditioned** responses longer than easily trainable animals such as cats or rabbits.

Bottom-dwelling spotted dogfish are popular with sport fishermen.

If a sand tiger shark is approached too closely, it will thump its tail forcefully, creating a booming sound to scare off aggressors.

Research shows that sharks are highly resistant to most diseases, including cancer. In the mid-1980s, scientists at the Mote Marine Laboratory in Florida conducted a series of experiments on sharks, injecting cancer-causing material into them. But the sharks remained healthy. Today, researchers are hoping to uncover the mystery of sharks' resistance to disease and apply that knowledge to help humans.

A chemical found in the spiny dogfish is already being tested on humans as a possible drug that could be used to prevent certain types of cancer from spreading through the human body. The substance is called "squalamine," after the dogfish's scientific name, *Squalus acanthias*. Unfortunately, current practices of overfishing put dogfishes and many other sharks at risk of disappearing from the oceans. They may be gone before they can reveal their medical secrets.

Public awareness of the value of sharks continues to grow. With every scientific discovery that is made about sharks, another myth is proven wrong. Today, rather than being fearful of sharks, many people are now interested in learning more about them and are willing to appreciate the important role these fascinating creatures play on Earth.

Large but non-aggressive gray reef sharks draw in divers, who find the sharks curious and easy to study.

ANIMAL TALE: KALAHIKI, THE SHARK GOD

Hawaiian culture is tied to the ocean and its creatures. The people of *Hawaii Nei*, or "Beloved Hawaii," the ancient land, believed in many gods, including Kamohoali'i, the shark god. He was named Kalahiki by the people who lived on the island of Maui. The story of Kalahiki illustrates the relationship between fishermen and sharks in Hawaiian tradition.

Kalahiki, a huge shark, enjoyed swimming in the deep, blue waters around Maui. His favorite place was a narrow strait with swift, roaring waves between Maui and the tiny island of Kaho'olawe. The people of Hawaii Nei considered this island to be *tapu*, or sacred—so sacred, in fact, that no human could even approach it.

One day, a fisherman decided that his son was now old enough to join him in fishing. With nets and harpoons stowed and ready, the fisherman and his son set out in their canoe to search for food. Their favorite kinds of fish were ahi, kumu, and manini.

They fished for many hours but caught nothing. A storm was brewing on the horizon, and all of the fish were moving to deeper water. The fisherman and his son followed the fish farther out to sea. They planned to catch enough fish for supper and then hurry home before the storm arrived.

The storm moved quickly, though, and with it came a strong wind that pushed the canoe toward the island of Kaho'olawe. The wind whirled, and the sky grew darker and darker. A heavy mist covered the surface of the sea. The fisherman and his son could no longer see land. They were lost.

As the sea raged, the fisherman held his son to protect him from being swept overboard. Then they saw it: a huge fin broke through the surface of the water and began to circle the canoe. It was a shark. The boy began to cry, his tears falling into the deep, blue water.

The shark raised its head above the waves. That's when the fisherman saw that this was no ordinary shark; it was Kalahiki, the shark god.

"Who spills tears into my sea?" Kalahiki called out to the fisherman. "You have never feared the sea before. Why now?"

"I fear not," replied the fisherman, "but my son has never experienced such a storm on the sea. We are lost, and he is afraid."

"I will help you," said Kalahiki, "but I want something in return."

The fisherman had caught no fish that day, so he had none to give to Kalahiki. All he had on board the canoe was awa, a bitter root used to make a powerful drink that helped the fisherman stay alert while fishing all day. He offered Kalahiki a taste. Kalahiki tasted the awa and was pleased with its pungent flavor.

"Give me some more," he said.

The fisherman complied. Then Kalahiki swam to the front of the canoe and shook his tail. The waves calmed, the wind subsided, and the mist lifted.

"Now I will show you the way to your island," Kalahiki said, and he led the fisherman and his son home safely.

Even today, Hawiian tradition calls for fishermen to always carry awa, or kava, with them when they fish—just in case they get lost and need to ask Kalahiki to show them the way home.

GLOSSARY

adapted – changed to improve its chances of survival in its environment

brackish – containing a mixture of salt water and fresh water

buoyancy – the ability to float in water

camouflage – the ability to hide, due to coloring or markings that blend in with a given environment

cartilage – firm, flexible body tissue

commercial – used for business and to gain a profit rather than for personal reasons

conditioned – made to respond or behave in a certain way as a result of training

DNA – deoxyribonucleic acid, a substance found in every living thing that determines the species and individual characteristics of that thing

ecosystem – a community of organisms, plants, and animals that live together in an environment

electromagnetic – describing the interrelation of magnetic fields and electrical currents, or electricity

estuaries – the mouths of large rivers, where the tides (from oceans or seas) meet the streams

evolved – gradually developed into a new form

extinction – the act or process of becoming extinct; coming to an end or dying out

gestation – the period of time it takes a baby to develop inside a mother's womb

metabolisms – processes that keep a body alive, including making use of food for energy

oceanographer – a scientist who studies the ocean and its inhabitants

parasites – animals or plants that live on or inside another living thing (called a host) while giving nothing back to the host; some parasites cause disease or even death

satellite – using information collected by a mechanical device launched into space

symbiotic – a kind of relationship between two living things that is good for both

SELECTED BIBLIOGRAPHY

Allen, Thomas B. *The Shark Almanac: A Fully Illustrated Natural History of Sharks, Skates, and Rays.* Guilford, Conn.: Lyons Press, 2003.

Benchley, Peter. *Shark Trouble.* New York: Random House, 2002.

Compagno, Leonard. *Sharks of the World.* Princeton, N.J.: Princeton University Press, 2005.

McGovern, Ann. *America's Shark Lady: The Complete Adventures of Eugenie Clark.* New York: Scholastic, 2004.

Pelagic Shark Research Foundation. "Homepage." Pelagic Shark Research Foundation. http://www.pelagic.org.

Shark Alliance. "Homepage." The Shark Alliance. http://www.sharkalliance.org.

Many sharks travel great distances to follow migrating schools of fish and thus have a ready food source.

INDEX